Over 50?
MeNopauSaL?
You're Fired!!!

By: Roni Elayne Singer
Nancy DePrimo Zuromski

STELLAR
COMMUNICATIONS
HOUSTON

Praise for the book

"What a great book! Spot-on illustrations and great tips for getting back on track."
  —Rhonda G., Therapist

"A candid, laugh-out-loud, uplifting book. Takes one's mind off the stress of being out of work."
  —Andrea L., MBA, MS, LCDC, AAC, BCI

"Penny Pinkslip turns adversity into the perfect 'how-to-get-re-employed' guide, navigating the murky world of unemployment back into the sanity of a fabulous new job!"
  —Tom Adkins, Television Producer

"Couldn't stop reading! By the end I was totally rooting for Penny Pinkslip!"
  —Olha Hirka, Writer, Houston Independent School District

"I feel transformed after reading these words. It's like my Enron days, waking up thinking I had somewhere to go and then realizing not. Happened to me!"
  —Erin Wesling, Senior Vice President

"Witty, insightful, informative! Penny Pinkslip reflects our years of hard work and the new job-hunting processes that ain't like they used to be. LOL!"
  —Nelia Hinojosa, Contract Sales, Distribution NOW

"Humorous, refreshing, helpful in surviving depression caused by unemployment."
  —Anne Guidace, Medical Assistant

"Illustrates the plight of the working class today and the tactics that dehumanize employees."
  —Giro G., Teacher

"Having had the honor of being a member of the 'over 50, you're outta here club,' the emotional roller coaster ride described in this book is spot on (sans the menopause)."
  —Carl F., Consultant

"A practical guide for someone going through job loss. You're not alone – there's hope!"
  —Peggy Williamson, Career Counselor

"A delightful resource for job seekers."
  —Nory Angel, Executive Director & CEO, SER - Jobs for Progress - Texas Gulf Coast

Dedication

This book is dedicated to all those who are or were at one time unemployed – not by choice. Whether you are male or female, young or not-so-young, blue collar or white collar, executive level or entry level, we understand and feel your pain. We also know that with a lot of hard work, a great support system and a positive attitude you'll pull through this better than ever.

Over 50?

Menopausal?

You're Fired!!!

For information, contact Stellar Communications Houston at www.stellarwriter.com.

Published by Stellar Communications Houston
www.stellarwriter.com
281-804-7089

ISBN 978-1-944952-12-9
E-book ISBN 978-1-944952-15-0

Project Conceived, & Written by: **Roni Elayne Singer**
Nancy DePrimo Zuromski
Illustrator: **Kathy Kopp**
Design/Production: **Arynne Elfenbein**

CONTENTS

CHAPTER 1

Introduction

HELLO, MY NAME IS PENNY PINKSLIP. I am a single, independent, mid-fifties, menopausal woman of average height, fluctuating dress-size, dishwater blonde hair, blue eyes, and a warm, friendly smile.

My 20+ years as an Executive Assistant, supporting **CEOs**, **CFOs**, **COOs**, **CIOs**, **CTOs** and **CPOs** (not to be confused with the Star Wars **C–3PO**) have qualified me to handle just about any situation that can possibly happen in the corporate world. My yearly reviews consistently exceeded expectations; I was well respected by my peers, available at the drop of a hat, and was known for making the best pumpkin pie during our annual Thanksgiving luncheons.

If you are reading this book, perhaps your career has taken the same unforeseen downturn as mine. Whether you have been dismissed, received notice, discharged, sacked, discontinued, no longer needed, terminated, let go, given the ol' heave-ho, released, let loose, repositioned, canned, axed, given the boot, relieved of duty, kicked out, unwaged, pink-slipped or laid off, I am here to tell you that there is life beyond "You're Fired!"

2

CHAPTER 2

And So It Begins...

REPORTING TO WORK AT THE WEADONT CARE COMPANY WHERE I'VE BEEN HAPPILY EMPLOYED FOR MANY YEARS, I grab a cup of strong coffee, strike up some chit-chat with several fellow co-workers and head off to my 4' x 6' cubicle. Settling into my comfy chair, I boot up my computer and BAM! The following message flashes on my screen:

"YOU ARE NO LONGER AUTHORIZED TO ACCESS THIS COMPUTER— CONTACT YOUR TECHNICAL ADMINISTRATOR."

And so it begins...

My boss – a/k/a 'The All Mighty' – commands, "I need to see you in my office!" As I walk the dreaded path to the holder of my destiny, I realize with just those few words my entire life is about to change. "Have a seat, Ms. Pinkslip," he says as he waves his hand toward a chair at the front of his desk. As I hesitantly walk toward the seat, I realize one of my many hot flashes has decided to appear at this very moment.

So, not only am I sweating due to fear of what's to come but I'm also burning up from the inside out due to a furnace of hormonal activity. Still, I try to remain calm and collected as I lower myself down in the chair that I've never actually sat in, but often straightened. "As you know, our company has been going through many changes in the past few months," he begins. I can see that he's uncomfortable speaking with me and avoids looking me in the eye as he stares at the perspiration stains that have now appeared under my arms.

"I have just been informed that the merger with Faultless-Union Incorporated, also known as FU Inc. has been finalized. They are bringing in their own employees, therefore, creating duplicate roles." From that point on all I hear is "blah, blah, blah… and so I'm going to have to let you go."

Let me go? Let me go where? To another department? To another office location? To another floor? No, he actually said the words. "Today is your last day here."

OH S#*T! I'm no longer wanted here. My expert services are not needed.

I JUST LOST MY JOB!

So, what exactly does that mean? I didn't really lose my job – I know exactly where it is. I can even see it from the window of the prison from which I am being sentenced. It's in the exact spot where I left it along with my desk, my chair, my pens, my phone, my personalized mouse pad, my family pictures, and my Post-It Notes, all of which I am no longer worthy to use and call my own. I didn't lose my job; my job lost me!

Sitting in a state of numbness, I didn't hear the rest of what my now-former-boss said. Something about me being a hard worker and loyal employee, that it was a difficult decision but someone has to go and he wishes things could be different, yada, yada, yada. I'm not really listening anymore. My mind is now trying to decipher if this is really happening or if it's all just a bad dream. I leave his office with my head hung low and the back of my dress drenched in sweat matching my arm pits.

OVER FIFTY? MENOPAUSAL? YOU'RE FIRED!!!

OVER FIFTY? MENOPAUSAL? YOU'RE FIRED!!!

I dejectedly walk back into what used to be my cubicle, pondering my grim future. Within seconds, as if expertly choreographed, a person from Human Resources appears. Her sole responsibility this morning is to personally escort me from my former cube out the door, reinforcing that I am no longer a trusted or needed employee of Weadont Care Company. She commands me to hand over my electronic key-card, my parking pass, the keys to the bathroom and supply room, and to start packing up my personal belongings.

This HR person, whom I never knew existed before, drops assorted empty cartons on the floor near my desk with a thud. Taking a firm stance that would make a Marine Corp Drill Sargent or Prison Warden proud, she carefully scrutinizes me as I place all of my personal possessions into the boxes ensuring that I don't accidentally take the corporate stapler, document holder, pens, paper clips or scissors that were entrusted to me upon my hiring.

Emotions flood in causing further embarrassment and confusion.

What did I do wrong?

Why are they portraying me like a criminal, after all the years that I've faithfully committed to this company? Why am I suddenly no longer trusted to delete my personal files from my computer or to leave the building on my own accord?

Why am I not even allowed to say goodbye to my colleagues with whom I've been working for so many years?

I am officially demeaned.

The Escorting-You-Out-Of-The-Building process is deeply humiliating. Catching sight of everyone nearby watching and whispering to each other about the upheaval, at what used to be Penny's desk, is mortifying.

As I'm being led away from my area the misery hits. It's as though I'm a 'dead woman walking' character, staggering toward death row. Convicted of a crime I did not commit. My legs are shaking and my knees are weak as I take one step at a

OVER FIFTY? MENOPAUSAL? YOU'RE FIRED!!!

time toward the company doors. I was tried in a fictitious court and condemned by executives who never knew I even existed until they dropped the gavel and sentenced me to the horrid nightmare of the unemployed. I feel myself walking in a trance, with slow, unsteady steps as if I'm bound in handcuffs and leg irons, toward the exit of the office. While trying to balance all of my boxes containing my personal items, I am desperately hoping that someone will burst in with a last-minute pardon. The HR person diligently walks one step behind me and one step to the left ensuring I don't do anything drastic while my mind is screaming, *this can't be happening to me!*

The atmosphere is heavy by the judgmental stares of everyone in the office looking at me out of the corner of their eye, trying not to make direct eye contact yet curious as to what is happening. Led through the corridors, passing friends and co-workers' offices and cubicles, I am forced to step over the threshold that puts me on the other side of Weadont Care Company's giant doors. My body shudders by the WHOOSH of the door, forever electronically locking behind me. Slowly turning around, I realize this is a physical separation, their final indignity that has been thrust upon me. My fate has been decided; there is no turning back. I'm now jobless and damned to the land of unemployment.

I stagger through the parking lot trying to hide behind my cartons and plants that once sat proudly on my desk. I realize that I am completely alone. The parking lot is eerily quiet with the exception of the echoes of my heels on the concrete. Sure, of course it's quiet. Its ten o'clock in the morning! Everyone else is working. Everyone else is employed. Everyone else has a job.

I find my car and dump in my possessions. In my head I tell myself *maybe it's for the best* or *it's their loss* or *perhaps it was meant to be*. None of these clichés make me feel better. As I settle into my car I look around to ensure no one is watching. And I cry.

CHAPTER 3

You're Home Now

STILL IN SHOCK, I ABSENT-MINDEDLY DRIVE HOME – WHERE ELSE WOULD I GO? It's odd walking into my house in the middle of the day. It's still light outside and I don't have the company computer bag rolling behind me, which for years I've always brought home in case my assistance was needed in the evening or the weekends.

Quickly logging into my personal computer, I email a few of my co-worker friends telling them what happened – in case they are looking for me. I want them to know about the injustice that was thrust upon me today and that I was pronounced guilty without cause. It is important they understand this early demise wasn't due to anything I did and is completely unwarranted. I am hoping for their sympathy and for them to be on my side although in my mind I know it is futile. In reality, they are all breathing a sigh of relief because it was not one of them being escorted out of the building. Even so, I tell myself that wallowing in self-pity is an acceptable thing to do at this point. I immediately receive replies from the co-workers I've emailed. Each message is filled with carefully worded outrage and genuine sadness. All of the emails contain similar statements: 'This is so sad;' 'Call me if you need anything;' 'I can't believe this happened to you'; 'This place won't be the same without you', and the inevitable 'We must get together for lunch soon.' With each passing hour, the emails and calls from my well-wishers become fewer and fewer. I anxiously hit the refresh button over and over again begging for new emails of encouragement to pop in, but my In-box continues to read 'No New Messages.' *That's okay*, I tell myself. *Everyone is busy doing their jobs. I understand.* This mental thinking makes me feel better… sort of, not really, but I try to convince myself anyway.

As the day wears on, I endlessly watch the clock as if I am still tethered to my work desk. My brain rewinds over and over again with project deadlines that are due this week and I am saddened with the realization that these projects, which were once my responsibility and pride, have been reassigned to someone else to complete and receive credit. Once again, my mental thinking kicks in: *Good luck giving my project to Susie. She doesn't know the meaning of a deadline. She hasn't hit a deadline in four years! She barely gets herself to work on time. Nice try giving it to Tom. My project will interfere with his internet search for the perfect date.*

And then it strikes me. These projects are no longer my projects or my concern. The responsibility of it can be taken off of my shoulders. For a brief moment, I begin to feel the stress of the day start to fade away. Bedtime beckons. Although I am mentally and physically exhausted, sleep does not come easily. My mind replays the morning scenario over and over and over again as I drift off to a restless sleep.

OH NO! I'm late! My alarm didn't go off! Jumping out of bed, I rush into the shower. As soap runs into my eyes, reality hits me like a ton of bricks. I am not late for anything. I don't have a job; I am no longer employed.

OVER FIFTY? MENOPAUSAL? YOU'RE FIRED!!!

OVER FIFTY? MENOPAUSAL? YOU'RE FIRED!!!

CHAPTER 4

Five Stages of Losing Your Job

WHEN EXPERIENCING THE DEATH OF A LOVED ONE, MOST PEOPLE ENDURE THE FIVE STAGES OF LOSS: Denial, Anger, Bargaining, Depression and Acceptance. Losing your job also has five stages of loss. They are as follows:

STAGE ONE **Denial** – In this first stage, you have a difficult time accepting that this is really happening to you. You replay the final scene of your employment over and over again in your mind hoping that there is some sort of mistake or that you'll wake up from this horrific, bad dream. Some of the things you'll be saying out loud or to yourself are: *This can't be happening. I've been doing such a good job. Surely this is a mistake. I thought my boss and I were friends. My co-workers are like my family. I've been with the company for so many years. I thought they loved me there. How can this happen?*

STAGE TWO **Loss of Self-Worth** (part 1) – After admitting to yourself that you really are no longer employed, feelings of sorrow and self-evaluation set in. You may think: *I'll never find another job. I can't compete with those younger people. Who's going to want to hire me? I'm such a failure. I'm too old to start all over again. How will I put 20+*

years of experience on a two-page resume? It's been years since I've been on an interview. I'm just too tired and depressed to look for another job. How will I pay my bills? Or worse, What if I'm not able to find employment again?

*WARNING: If several days pass and you just can't get out of bed, contact a professional. This is not something to be embarrassed about. This is the time to take care of **YOU!**

STAGE THREE   **Acceptance** – After some time, you begin to get your 'old self' back again. Your confidence level improves and you start working toward getting a better job or career than the one you had before. You may say to yourself: *Okay, they are not going to ask me to come back. I can do this. I can find another job. It's all gonna be okay. I've done it before and I'll do it again. I always land on my feet. I'm like a cat with nine lives! In the middle of every difficulty lies opportunity. This too shall pass!*

STAGE FOUR   **Loss of Self-worth** (part 2) – Time goes by and hundreds of resumes go out and you're once again in the Loss of Self-worth stage. You begin to realize that your resume is no longer ready for electronic uploading and you need to update your credentials. In addition, you now need to brush up on those interviewing skills. *Wow, those interviews are not like I remember them. The people interviewing me are so young. They could be my children. This is too hard. I can't believe I'm actually in this situation. Look at all these questions they are asking on the application. I don't fit into any of these requirements. I don't understand how I should answer their questions.* It's normal to feel this way.

STAGE FIVE   **Jubilation** – This is the final step, the one each and every unemployed person dreams of achieving. Somewhere, in the jumbled maze of companies scattered throughout the metropolitan area, a brilliant HR genius thinks you're a perfect fit. In that person's unlimited wisdom, you are the older generation, with years of experience, and it's actually a good thing. In fact, it's a great thing! Your confidence level is now restored and you're standing proud. *Hey, someone actually wants to hire me. This is going* *to be a great change for me. I'm looking forward to doing something new. I can't wait to start my new career. Somebody needs me, they really need me. I know I can do it!*

Although the little tiny voice in the back of your head is whispering, *I hope I don't get terminated again.*

CHAPTER 5

Things to Do While Out of Work

I N THE BEGINNING, BEING OUT OF WORK CAN BE A GOOD THING. You don't have to get up early and you can lounge around in your PJ's for as long as you'd like. You may even laugh at those who are stuck in traffic as you roll over in bed. Suddenly you have hours of freedom. You can now catch up on the 1,497 tasks you could not finish before because you held down a 9-hour-a-day job.

Give yourself permission to feel sorrow. You've earned the right to ask yourself, *Why me? Why not Bob* or *Mary* or *Bruce?* You're also allowed to elaborate on that question by thinking, *Bob is an idiot. He doesn't do half the work I do, so why is he still there and I'm not?* Or, *Mary actually made two clients cry last week, why does she still have a job and I don't?* Or, *Bruce, that brown-noser who can hardly spell his name without spell-check... why is he still getting a paycheck?* You do need to realize that there are no answers to these questions because, you will tell yourself, *Weadont Care Company obviously doesn't have a clue of the mistake they've made, otherwise, they wouldn't have let me go!*

OVER FIFTY? MENOPAUSAL? YOU'RE FIRED!!!

MUST-DO TASKS DURING THE FIRST WEEK OF UNEMPLOYMENT:

1. Apply for Unemployment Benefits

Immediately apply for your unemployment benefits from the Workforce Commission of your state. Be prepared to expect a call from your state unemployment representative questioning the motive of your former employers' decision such as, "Is it true that you were let go due to the merger with FU Inc.?" "Yes," I softly reply, "that is exactly what my employer told me was the reason for my termination." After a lengthy, deafening pause on the other end, I am told my meager severance benefits are approved.

2. Re-evaluate Your Spending

Since unemployment payments are only a fraction of your previous salary, it is now time to review your expenses, create a budget and re-evaluate your spending habits. Whether or not you have received a severance package, you must change your thinking and realize that your money may run out before you actually find a new job. You must learn how to stretch your finances within the means of the unemployment benefits you will be receiving. Gone are the days of paying full price at Macy's or daily double-mocha lattes at Starbucks. Now are the days of clipping coupons, scouting for sales, bargain basement blue-light specials at K-Mart, and yes, Dollar Days at the Dollar Store. Now is also the time to cut up your credit cards or take them out of your wallet to avoid self-pity, spur-of-the-moment, unbudgeted shopping.

3. Schedule Doctor Appointments and Refill Prescriptions NOW!

If you already have insurance through your employer, most companies will provide medical, dental, vision and prescription coverage through the end of the current month of giving you the boot. Be sure to utilize your benefits to the max before they expire. Been dreading that mammogram? Schedule it now. Need refills of your maintenance drugs? Get them filled immediately and try to get a 90-day supply, if possible. Been needing to get that crown fixed, but didn't want to make the time?

Do it now and have the dentist check for any other oral needs you may require. Need new contacts or glasses? Schedule the appointment as soon as possible. Glasses and contacts often take a couple of weeks to be ready. Cram in as many appointments as you can in the time you have left. In other words, have your doctors check every nook and cranny of your body to make sure no surprises are lurking. If they are, get them fixed while you're still covered. Also, be sure to check into COBRA through your previous company.

4. Update Your Resume

Job searching is not like it used to be. Once upon a time someone would actually read your resume, decide if your skills match the job description, then offer you a position on the spot.

Nowadays, your resume's only mission is to get you the interview. The resume tells the potential employer that according to your skills you "may" be a good fit. But will you "fit" into their office culture too? Hence the interview.

In some cases, it's been a long time since you've looked at your resume. Update your last position by listing your previous responsibilities. And be sure to change "currently employed" with the appropriate end-date. Review the entire resume to ensure all necessary key-words are present. It's good to brag about your accomplishments; however, be aware that your skills must match your successes. Be accurate; they will check and they will find out!

You may find that with your vast years of experience, you fit in several job categories. For example, as an Executive Assistant, I am also an Office Manager as well as a very skilled travel organizer. Therefore, I have several resumes, each one highlighting the different areas of expertise of which I am applying. Just be sure to remember which resume you sent to whom and for which position.

5. The Job Hunt

Create a daily routine and stick with it. Begin your job hunting day at the same time you used to start your work day. Take breaks, stop for lunch and end your day at the normal time. Do not make your search all encompassing. Turn off the computer at the end of the day and allow yourself to relax.

Weeding through the want-ads either in the newspaper or online is a daunting task. Unless you're a CPA or a fireman, you have to be creative when looking for a job title that fits your skills. As an Executive Assistant with 20+ years of experience I am surprised to find that my skill-set fits into numerous job titles such as Executive Administrative Assistant, Senior Office Manager, Senior Administrator, Administrator Assistant III, Office Executive Administrator, Executive Secretary, Administrator Coordinator, and Executive Office Administrator. All are the same position but with a different label. Unfortunately, many companies hire lower-level positions, but require upper-level skills in order to avoid paying bigger salaries. Or the company is only hiring for part-time in order to avoid paying insurance and other company benefits.

It is important to itemize your experience instead of grouping your skills into one. For example, if your previous responsibilities included assistance to the company accountant with your accounts payable skills, be sure to highlight this additional talent. Perhaps you've become an expert at international travel arrangements. Be sure to highlight this as a skill as well.

6. Professional Networking

You know the old saying, "It's not what you know but who you know." In today's job search, this old cliché couldn't be truer. It's not enough to search the job boards or want-ads, you have to know someone. Many times, jobs are found by meeting someone, talking to them about what you do, getting to know them and then deciding they need someone like you to work for them.

Also, knowing someone can help bypass the somewhat unknowing Human Resources recruiter and, worst of all, the dreaded Automatic Tracking System (ATS).

Most companies have a Human Resources Department where someone has the task of finding the right person for a particular position. In many cases, the HR Recruiter has no clue what the job entails and usually they have only a checklist of what to look for in a potential candidate. Trying to explain your skills as a Senior Programmer Analyst specializing in Visual Basic.NET and C++ programming languages is like talking to someone in English who only knows how to speak Finnish. It may be necessary to dumb-down your responses, just to get past the first phase of the process.

The ATS is a frustrating and, in my opinion, unfair practice. It's designed to electronically "read" your resume and dispose of the ones that don't have the correct keywords, education level, and/or skills. It's a computer with no emotions and no human interaction. There is no discussion or communication. Your resume either passes this step or is tossed out without any explanation.

This is why knowing someone, or knowing someone who knows someone, is often your best bet. That special someone can personally walk your resume directly to the hiring manager and directly place it in the hands of the decision maker.

Networking gatherings can be very unnerving. Within a 30-seconds-or-less prepared speech, you need to introduce yourself, tell someone what you do, what skills you possess and what you're looking for... all without making it sound like you're desperate or needy. This is what the networking professionals call 'an elevator speech'. It needs to sound like ordinary conversation but there is nothing ordinary about it. Normally, you would never have this type of conversation with someone you've just met but at networking events, it's not only expected, it's required.

While this is the preferred method of finding your next opportunity, it's not as simple as it sounds. If you're not a natural born extravert, then networking might be a little intimidating. Picture yourself walking into a group of strangers gathered at some professional networking event, making small talk with anyone and everyone because you never know who knows someone who could help you in your search.

By the time you are done, your face hurts from perpetually smiling and pretending to be interested in what they have to say. When you finally return to the quiet of your car, it will strike you that job hunting is more difficult than actually working. Take a deep breath, make notes of the names, phone numbers and conversations you want to follow up on, and then relax the muscles in your face.

Another note: networking people do not refer to themselves as 'unemployed'. They prefer the term 'in transition'. To me, 'in transition' is just a nicer and more formal way of saying 'unemployed'. It's kind of like saying the words 'domestic engineer' instead of 'maid'.

On the plus side of networking, you might meet some really interesting people. I've actually made some very nice, long-lasting friends. But on the negative side, it can be overwhelming, humiliating, nerve-racking, anxiety-ridden, exhausting, and just plain uncomfortable. Nevertheless, it's an extremely important part of the job search so take a deep breath, arm yourself with your new updated resumes and business cards, place a confident smile on your face and jump in.

The flip side of being unemployed is that you now have time to do all of the things you've wanted to do but couldn't, because you were dedicating yourself to the company that supposedly valued you so much. Now you can make your days, nights and weekends your own. Being unemployed doesn't have to be all depressing and all doom-and-gloom 24/7.

THE LIGHTER SIDE OF UNEMPLOYMENT CAN BE FUN-EMPLOYMENT!

Here Are Some Suggestions:

1. Daily To-Do List

Try to stretch your weekend errands to be done during the normal work week. For example, let's say you used to create a food menu on a Sunday, and buy everything needed for a week's worth of dinners. Now, armed with money-saving coupons, you can go to your favorite grocery store every day for the dinner you'll be cooking each night. By going grocery shopping each day, you get to run a meaningful errand. This gives you a reason to get out of bed, get dressed and have a purpose for the day.

2. Organize

Clean out a drawer or closet. I have re-arranged several drawers and cabinets in my kitchen and some of them have been done more than once. This task is time consuming, mind numbing and gives you an excuse to go to the Dollar Store to buy inexpensive, pretty containers and dividers when reorganizing your drawers and cabinets, providing yet another important task to do during the work day.

3. Clean, Clean, Clean

I mean really clean. We all do the basic dusting and vacuuming but now you have the time to do a truly thorough cleaning.

- Push aside some of the furniture and unearth the collection of debris along with that bologna sandwich you lost two years ago.

- Scour that waxy, yellow build-up on your kitchen floor and melt it down to make yourself a new candle (another money-saving tip).

- Scrape off those layers of dirty film on the windows and screens that you told yourself provided a helpful filter against harmful and aging rays from the sun.

- Sweep up the dust bunnies that have nested and reproduced underneath your bed.

- Get rid of the hidden cobwebs that have claimed squatter's rights in the corners of your living room.

- Vacuum up the pet hair on the cushions of your couch and discover that your couch color is really white and not gray.

4. Learn New Skills

Teach yourself a new skill. Last year a friend bought me a wonderful camera. I had no clue how to use all of the settings and gadgets so it sat in my drawer. Now that I have extra time, I am actually reading the owner's manual. As of this writing, I have photographed over 350 shots of my cat in various sleeping positions.

Contact your local community college to inquire about classes. If you have no desire to brush up on work skills, look into non-credited classes such as writing, cake decorating, or growing a garden. Learning a new skill will boost your self-esteem. It is also an excellent way to meet new people. Often community colleges are looking for people who possess unique talents such as canning, photography, quilting, etc. Perhaps you would like to become a part-time instructor? This will get you out of the house, add some income to your finances and may lead to a new career path.

5. Volunteer

Volunteering is a perfect way to make new connections, keep up your skills, learn a new skill, and give back to your community.

Dedicating your time as a volunteer can:
- Help you make new friends
- Expand your professional network
- Boost your social skills
- Increase self-confidence
- Combat depression
- Help you stay physically healthy
- Provide career experience
- Teach you valuable future job skills.

Try to find a charity that is flexible so that you can continue your job search. Also, try to find a charity that is in line with your career. For example, since I am an Executive Assistant, I volunteer at an organization where I answer the phones, take notes and type letters for the executives a few hours a week and do as much office work as needed. This looks great on my resume as it shows that although I'm not being paid for my time and skills, at least I'm keeping them current. A plus for volunteering: they might think you're so good that they hire you full-time with a real paycheck and benefits!

6. Begin a New Hobby

Start or re-start a hobby. If you used to knit, play the piano, paint, or if there is a project that you've been putting off due to lack of time, do it now. It will take your mind off of the fact that it's the middle of the week in the middle of the day and you're at home. Once you've accomplished this task and created something to be proud of, you'll feel great.

7. Exercise

If you're not already an exercise buff, now is a good time to start a routine. Since you're not in the office you're probably spending more time just hanging around the house, eating the new gastronomical masterpieces that you made with all the time off you have. In that case, you might as well hang around outside. Start walking or running or punching a bag (picture your former boss's face on it!). It can help get your frustrations out during this stressful time of job searching. In addition, it will distance you from the high-calorie snacks beckoning you to consume them. Do not use this time to sign up at an expensive gym or spa. You can lose the weight without losing the cash.

30

8. Relax and Read

Catch up on your reading. Dust off those books and magazines that have been piling up. The uninterrupted peace and quiet during the day is a welcome change.
*WARNING: Avoid snacking on chips and candy while reading.

9. Treat Yourself

If it's in your budget, allow yourself to go see that chick–flick movie you've always wanted to see but never had the time. Since it's during the day, tickets are a lot cheaper. Another money-saving tip: If you go to the movies, pack some snacks in a big bag. This way, you won't have to pay for those high–dollar bags of popcorn sold at the theatre.

Things To Watch Out For:

- **Beware of Weight Gain**

  If you like to cook, try new cuisines or exotic recipes. Since being terminated, my family, including my extended family and friends, have gained several pounds taste-testing all of my experimental cooking sensations. Try to minimize the caloric intake. Gaining weight will only add to your sadness of being unemployed and fat!

- **New Found Freedom**

  Don't think you need to be job searching eight hours a day, five days a week (including holidays) while everyone else is actually working and earning a paycheck. There is only so much one can do in a given week. Therefore, this frees up more time to do things you normally could not do in the middle of the day in the middle of the work week. Although you may feel pangs of guilt when doing something you actually enjoy between the hours of 8 a.m. and 5 p.m. Monday through Friday, keep in mind this situation was forced upon you through no fault of your own. Important note: This free time and feelings of sadness does not give you permission to go shopping!

CHAPTER 6
Family and Friends (F&F)

FAMILY AND FRIENDS ARE VERY IMPORTANT DURING THIS TIME SO BE SURE TO MAKE USE OF THEM. I believe all of my F&F genuinely feel sad for me. They all have said at one time or another, "Keep your chin up, there's a light at the end of the tunnel" (I'm hoping it's not a speeding freight train), or "When one door closes, another one opens". Unfortunately, those words don't fill the void I am feeling... or pay my overdue bills. When hearing these enlightening phrases from these sincere-meaning people, it is important that you smile and let them know how much you appreciate their support even though inside you feel like screaming.

Also, you might hear one of your F&F suggest, "Why don't you do something different and start a whole new career?" Well, if you're under the age of 40 that may be a good idea. You can go back to school or take an entry-level position for a few years until you are experienced enough to pursue a more seasoned level.

But, if you're of the age of 50++, this is not really feasible. By the time you finish with school and then accept an entry-level, minimum wage position because you don't have the experience yet, you'll be ready to retire. I suppose if you're financially secure and money is not a problem, then by all means, do it – go back to school. But if you're like most of us, that just won't work.

Always have your resume updated and readily available just in case someone mentions that they have a friend of a friend who might be able to help you find a new job, or that they know someone who might be able to use your skills. Therefore, you can cheerfully say thank you and immediately hand over your potential employment document. Submit your resume as often as possible to as many job listings as possible. Flood the workforce with that all-important piece of paper listing your talents. You never know who's going see it and think that you're a perfect fit.

Although you're sad and perhaps feeling a little worthless, try hard to fight these feelings and menopausal emotions and keep your spirits up when you're with your F&F. Just because YOU feel down and out, don't bring everyone else down with you. It's important to have hope at this stage of your unemployment. Keep in mind that F&F only want to help, so it's vital you keep your attitude positive not only for yourself but for them as well.

So, when someone says they are sorry to hear that you lost your job, you might want to politely correct them by saying, "I didn't lose my job, I know exactly where my job is – my job lost me!"

It's okay to ask F&F to NOT inquire on a daily basis the status of your job search. It's no fun repeating "no interviews are scheduled yet" or "no, I have not heard from the 2,000 jobs I've applied". F&F may suggest to take any job that comes along, just get your foot in the door. That's easier said than done and most likely, you will not be hired because you're overqualified. And in regard to getting one's foot in a door, be careful not to get your toes amputated because that proverbial door has a tendency to slam shut. Most importantly, don't let your F&F keep asking WHY you're not employed yet. Don't let them make you feel that YOU are doing something wrong. F&F will want to give you advice. But if they haven't been in the job market in the past four or five years, their advice will probably no longer be relevant. Job searching today is completely different than it was even a few years ago but there will be no way to satisfactorily explain this to them. Simply remind your F&F that you'll let them know when there is a new development. Note: When F&F do keep asking you these questions, they are really hoping for themselves that you will have good news to tell them because F&F really don't know how to handle situations such as this of which they have no control.

Try to keep your life with your F&F as normal as possible. If you used to meet your friends for dinner every third Thursday of the month, then Bon Appetite! (Remember to include this expense in your new budget.) Not only does it keep a little normalcy in your life, it gets you out of the house and away from the TV.

Better yet, invite your friends over for a pot luck meal. Create a menu and email it asking them to bring one of the dishes. By doing this it eliminates extra expense for you, and brings your friends together in a more relaxed atmosphere. If you're lucky you may even have some delicious leftovers to enjoy later in the week.

Speaking of the TV...

Just because you're spending more time at home, don't let the TV become your new best friend. Being unemployed makes it very easy to start up a secret affair with your Sony. If you can easily recite the TV schedule for any given day or time slot, then it's time for a major commercial break between you and your remote control.

Separation from your TV doesn't mean attaching yourself to your computer either. Use your computer only for emails and job searching and maybe a little game playing. Don't let your Dell become your new addiction.

Get yourself a rock. What I mean by this is someone who you can count on to laugh and cry with about your situation. In my case, I have my BFF Wanda Working. Wanda is always there with much needed advice and her support is unbounded. She lets me know that I will be okay and that this is not my fault. She lets me cry as needed and she cheers me up by telling me how horrible Weadont Care Company is. Having someone who is always there for you without question is a crucial necessity when in the unemployed state. A rock can be husband/wife, a best friend, a sister/brother, a mom/dad etc. Find yourself a rock and hold on tight.

OVER FIFTY? MENOPAUSAL? YOU'RE FIRED!!!

37

CHAPTER 7
TGIM (Thank God it's Monday)

MOST WORKING PEOPLE REJOICE TGIF AT THE END OF A WORK WEEK. They can't wait to get away from their desk and boss and spend a few leisurely days relaxing and doing something fun.

Those of us who are unemployed, hate Fridays! Fridays mean another week that has gone by with no job offers, another seven days that have disappeared with no prospects. It's very defeating. We, the unemployed, love Mondays. Mondays signify hope. The people who make the hiring decisions are at their desk looking for people like me. They have an itch and I can scratch it – they just don't know it yet.

Mondays bring optimism that this is a new week and something big is going to happen. Someone, somewhere is reading my resume and looking at their calendar to see the next available opening they have to meet me. Mondays bring faith that someone is on our side and life is going to get so much better. Mondays bring anticipation that soon – very soon – we won't have to collect any more unemployment pittance and we'll be able to cash a real paycheck.

On Monday mornings you make your follow-up calls and check the status of your previously submitted resumes. You ask to meet with the hiring manager. If you're lucky, you get to actually speak to someone within the company. Sometimes it's via phone and sometimes it's via e-mail. Either way, there is hope that something good will happen. Because it's Monday!

Don't get me wrong – Tuesdays, Wednesdays and Thursdays are good too for the reasons I stated above. But Fridays are bad. No one returns calls on Fridays and no big decisions are made on Fridays. Why? Because everyone in the workforce is only focusing on getting out of the office as soon as possible for the weekend. Hence – TGIF is for the working people and TGIM is for the unemployed.

40

CHAPTER 8

The Big Black Hole

I WAKE UP MY USUAL TIME—EARLY. I'm not able to sleep in. I roll out of bed, make a beeline to the bathroom and then brush my teeth. Pulling out my laptop, I log in, look for new job postings and follow-up with the positions I applied for last week.

It's Monday, a new week with new opportunities. I feel hopeful. I begin my search looking for advertised postings for an Executive Administrator, Senior Office Manager, Executive Assistant or any combination of titles that support my vast experience. Ah, here's one.

"REPORTING DIRECTLY TO THE VICE PRESIDENT FOR IT AND CIO, THE EXECUTIVE ASSISTANT (EA) PROVIDES EXECUTIVE SUPPORT IN A ONE-ON-ONE WORKING RELATIONSHIP. THE RESPONSIBILITIES OF THE EA INCLUDE, BUT ARE NOT LIMITED TO SERVING AS THE PRIMARY POINT OF CONTACT FOR INTERNAL AND EXTERNAL CONSTITUENCIES ON ALL MATTERS PERTAINING TO THE OFFICE OF THE CIO. THE EA ALSO SERVES AS A LIAISON; SCHEDULING AND CALENDARING MEETINGS; ORGANIZES AND COORDINATES OUTREACH AND EXTERNAL RELATIONS EFFORTS; AND OVERSEES SPECIAL PROJECTS. MINIMUM OF EIGHT (8) YEARS OF EXPERIENCE WITH DIRECT EXECUTIVE LEVEL SUPPORT. STRONG EXPERIENCE MANAGING

INTERNATIONAL TRAVEL ARRANGEMENTS; MUST HAVE KNOWLEDGE OF THE TRAVEL INDUSTRY AND BE ABLE TO WORK CLOSELY WITH OUR TRAVEL AGENCY."

That's me! It's screaming my name. I'm perfect for this job. I'm going to apply right now. I press the *"Apply Online"* button and up pops a long, lengthy and very detailed application form. Sighhh, been there, done that. Some applications are easy — answer one or two questions, attach your resume and ta-da, you're done. But most applications are specific and painstakingly meticulous to fill out.

It's 9:12 a.m. and I begin.

CONTACT INFORMATION
- Name – first, middle, last.
- Address – address1, address2, city, state, zip including the last four digits.
- If I lived at the above address less than 7 years, include additional addresses.
- Other Names Used, including maiden name.
- Primary Phone Number / Secondary Phone Number
- Email address / Re-enter email address
- Create user name
- Create password / Re-enter password
- Will you relocate?
    If yes, where?
- Will you agree to travel?
    If yes, what percentage of the time?
- Will you agree to a background check?
- Will you agree to random drug testing?
- Have you been convicted of a felony?
    If yes, please explain.
    …The thought crossed my mind as I was being escorted out of my last work place.

- Have you been convicted of a DUI?
    If yes, please explain.
- Have you ever been asked to leave a company?
    If yes, please explain.
    …Do they want my dress size and blood type too?

42

ATTACHMENTS

- Attach resume
- Attach cover letter
- Attach any other necessary documents

NEXT PAGE...

EMPLOYMENT

Enter every position held starting from current for the past 15 years.

- Company name
- Company address – address1, address2, city, state, zip, including last four digits
- Company Phone
- Job Title
- Date Started / Date Ended
- Salary Started / Salary Ended
- Bonus Amount (if applicable)
- Supervisor Name / Title / Phone / Email
- Can we contact your former supervisor? ☐ yes ☐ no
- Did You Manage Others?
    If so, how many?
- Reason for leaving
    ...I wish I knew.

This continues for five more previous companies.
   ...What's the point of attaching my resume if I have to fill all of this out manually anyway?

NEXT PAGE...

EDUCATION

- High School
- City / State of High School
- Year Started / Year Ended
- Did you graduate?
    ...Seriously? Did I graduate high school???

OVER FIFTY? MENOPAUSAL? YOU'RE FIRED!!!   43

COLLEGE/UNIVERSITY

- Name of College/University
- City / State of College/University
- Level Attained
- Field of Study - Major / Minor
- Did you graduate?
- Year started / Year ended College/University

  …Oh great, now they can figure out how old I am. Is this legal?

NEXT PAGE…

CERTIFICATIONS

- Name of Certification
- City / State of Certification
- Year started Certification
- Certification expiration date

NEXT PAGE…

REFERENCES

Enter at least three (3) references with one being a former supervisor.

- Reference Name / Title / Phone / Reference Email
- How do you know this reference?
- How long have you known this reference?

  …I hope they have something nice to say about me, …or at least make up a good story.

NEXT PAGE…

VOLUNTARY INFORMATION

- Race
- Sex

  …Not in a long time…oh, that's probably not what they mean.

- Protected Veteran?
- Disabled?

  …I'm feeling a bit disabled because this job searching is consuming my life!

LEGAL AGREEMENT

Ugh. Does anyone really read this? I have no idea what it says because some lawyer wrote it in a legal language that only members of the U.S. Supreme Court can interpret. For all I know, they are asking me to sell my first born male child. Nevertheless, unless I agree, I cannot continue with the application so I check the "ACCEPT" box.

ELECTRONICALLY SIGN AND DATE _____

NEXT PAGE...

REVIEW

I've spent over an hour filling out this application. At this point I don't care what it says. I assume I filled it out correctly and I'm sticking with it. I slide the mouse to the "Submit" button located at the bottom of the form.

It is now 10:24 a.m. and I click the button. The cursor spins as if it's processing and then the screen goes blank.

What happened? Where did it go? Oh no, is this supposed to happen? Something doesn't look right. I'm getting nervous.

Suddenly the screen flashes back and I'm right where I started, inviting me to apply.

I don't know if the application was submitted or if it has fallen into a black hole.

What choice do I have? Looking at the clock on my wall it reads 10:35 a.m. and I start all over again. This time when I hit the Submit button – 1 hour and 17 minutes later, I receive an automatic reply saying the application has been successfully received.

Leaning back in my chair, I breathe a sigh of relief. I need another cup of coffee.

I apply to three other companies, some submitted in under thirty seconds and some much, much longer.

I can't be sure where these applications and attachments go. I assume they are sent to the Human Resource's in-box of the company to which I applied, or perhaps their Junk Mail? I have no way of really knowing.

Now it's time for my follow-up calls. I Google each company trying to find a phone number, so I can talk to someone to find out the status of the applications I submitted last week.

Some companies are very friendly. They not only answer the phone when I call but they update me on the state of my application. Unfortunately, too many companies do not answer their phone, do not return my calls and will not give me a status or any information. It's as if they are telling me 'don't call us, we'll call you'. Message received, loud and clear. It's all somewhere in a big, black hole.

The Big Black Hole is the abyss, the great void, the missing sock from my dryer, Amelia Earhart's missing plane, the Bermuda Triangle of unemployment. Resumes, cover letters, phone calls, and emails go in, and are never heard from again. It's a hit or miss situation but since I don't know which one will hit and which one will miss, I have no choice but to follow up on each and every application I've submitted.

OVER FIFTY? MENOPAUSAL? YOU'RE FIRED!!!

CHAPTER 9

The Call

RRRRrrrrriiiinnnngggg. "Ms. Pinkslip, this is Olivia Opportunity from the Swindle and Konn Corporation and we'd like to bring you in for an interview. Are you available tomorrow at 9 a.m.?" Immediately my thoughts are drawn to all that I have to do tomorrow such as finishing organizing the hall closet, reading the last chapter of the latest love and lust novel and watching the last portion of 'The People's Court'. "Yes, I believe I am available tomorrow at 9:00am" you say with new-found excitement. After all necessary information is relayed, I hang up the phone and start jumping for joy. Wow, a real company wants to meet me.

OMG! What to wear? Running to my closet and tearing out every interview outfit I've ever owned, I simultaneously call my BFF Wanda Working for her professional advice.

Wanda appears at my door in record time and we sort each outfit into a good or bad pile. I notice the bad pile is dominated by clothes that no longer fit due to sampling those new dessert recipes.

Many important decisions have to be made at this time:

- Pantyhose or no pantyhose?
- Pantsuit or dress?
- V-neck or crew-neck?
- Dangle earrings or studs?
- Gold chain or pearls?
- Bright colors or shades of gray?
- Hair up or down?
- Perfume or au-natural?
- Full-face make-up or just a little blush?
- Heels or flats?

Sigh… men have it so easy – shower and shave and they're out the door.

We finally decide on the perfect outfit for my all-important interview. I also check several times that I have printed and memorized the directions to the interview and that I have extra copies of my resume and samples of my work. I will now spend the rest of the evening learning everything ever written about the company from their website and seeing who's who through LinkedIn.

It's time for bed. But sleep will not come easily. My head is replaying what they might ask me and how I can intelligently answer. I rehearse in my mind several forms of introductions and visualize how to sit confidently in that significant, life-changing chair.

OVER FIFTY? MENOPAUSAL? YOU'RE FIRED!!!

OVER FIFTY? MENOPAUSAL? YOU'RE FIRED!!!

CHAPTER 10

The Interview

THE ALARM SOUNDS PROMPTLY AT 7:00 A.M. BUT IT DOESN'T WAKE ME BECAUSE I'VE BEEN UP SINCE 4:30 A.M. After a quick shower, I carefully apply my make-up, style my hair and dress in the outfit that was so diligently selected. I try to eat something but my stomach is too tense to accept any food so I have a cup of tea instead.

It's time to go.

I check myself in the mirror for the hundredth time, make sure all copies of my resume and work samples are safely tucked into my portfolio. And I check myself in the mirror one more time. Out the door I go.

Driving carefully, I arrive at my destination, albeit 45 minutes too early. Oh no! Another hot flash! I turn the A/C blower to full-blast hoping to dry off. Time to go in. I try to stay calm and hope that my moist appearance doesn't make it seem as if I had just come from the gym. I take the elevator to the designated floor and walk up to the receptionist.

"Hello, my name is Penny Pinkslip and I have an appointment with Olivia Opportunity," I say with a little quiver in my voice.

"Yes, Ms. Pinkslip. Ms. Opportunity will be with you shortly. Please have a seat."

So, I sit and I wait for what feels like an eternity but it's really only a few minutes.

The receptionist walks over and tells me that Ms. Opportunity is ready to see me. Portfolio in hand, I follow her down the hallway. We stop at a doorway and there she is: The one person who can change my life forever. The one person who has the ability to accept or reject me. The one person who can make me and my bank account happy again. It's like seeing the Wizard from behind the curtain and the Wizard is going to give me a job! We shake hands and I silently hope she doesn't notice my sweaty palms. She offers me a seat in front of her giant oak desk. I carefully sit and decide on a position. Back straight, knees together but with legs crossed at the ankle. In my mind, it shows confidence. Or, does it appear that I have to use the bathroom - that "Depends".

The interview begins.

Olivia Opportunity (**OO**): "Welcome Penny. I found your resume to be quite interesting. You are very experienced and we need someone with your skills."

Penny Pinkslip (**PP**): "Oh, thank you. I enjoy learning new things and I like to keep myself up-to-date on new features as much as possible." Oh, my God, I think to myself, she really likes me. I'm doing great. Suddenly I hear my stomach growl. Did she hear it too?

OO: "So, Penny, tell me why you left your last employment."

PP: Uh-oh, I say to myself. "Well, Weadont Care Company merged with FU Inc., therefore duplicating positions," I reply.

OO: "Oh, so everyone in your department was laid off?"

PP: Geez, I think to myself before answering. How do I tell her that it was only me in my department? "No, not everyone, just a few," I say meekly. Okay, it's not really a lie because I am a part of a few.

OO: *"I see on your resume that you've used the Cook and Done 250 machine. We don't use that here; we use the Jones and Johnson 1090 machine. Are you familiar with that?"*

PP: *In my mind the voice says, Uh, no! Should I lie and say yes? I speak aloud, "No, I'm not." I've never even heard of the Jones and Johnson 1090 machine. If I blow this interview I'm going to have to get out my Smith and Wesson .45!*

OO: *"Are you familiar with the Quick Meeting RQ7 software? We use that when we set up internal meetings within our department".*

PP: *"Uh, no, I'm afraid not." There it goes, slipping through my fingers. BREATHE! BREATHE! BREATHE! Where IS my Smith and Wesson .45 anyway?*

OO: *"Have you ever used the AJ 2100 Phone System?"*

PP: *"Yes, yes I have used the AJ 2100 Phone System," I say beaming with pride and sitting up a little straighter now. "It is quite a sophisticated piece of equipment. We started using it two years ago and I trained everyone on how to use it." Yeah! I scored. She loves me. I'm sure to get the job now.*

OO: *"What are your goals for the next five years? Where do you see yourself?"*

PP: *After winning the lottery, touring the South Pacific on my yacht with a margarita in my hand…, I think to myself. "Well, in five years I hope to be an expert in my field and an asset to the company. I hope to grow within the company in order to maintain a status and a means of helping those around me to grow as well." That was so pathetic. As soon as I get home, I'm going to look for my Smith and Wesson.*

OO: *"Well, thank you for coming in to see us. You'll be hearing from us soon."*

And, it's over. It's done. I never got a chance to tell her my great accomplishments or let her know just how wonderful I really am and she doesn't even know about my award-winning pumpkin pie. I stand, we shake hands and smile and I walk out the door as my underwear clings to my body due to another hot flash and my urinary incontinence starts to trickle down my leg. Not really. But almost.

I head home so I can cry… again.

OVER FIFTY? MENOPAUSAL? YOU'RE FIRED!!!

58

CHAPTER 11
When It Rains, It Pours

ACTUALLY, WHEN YOU'RE UNEMPLOYED AND CRAPPY THINGS HAPPEN, IT'S MORE LIKE A TSUNAMI. As if being out of a job and out of money with no prospects on the horizon isn't bad enough, on the ride home from the interview I notice my car engine starting to smoke. *What the heck is this?* I say aloud to no one. I turn into the nearest service station and pull up to one of the garage bays.

A service mechanic comes out wiping his hands on a dirty rag. "What seems to be the problem?" he asks.

"My car suddenly started smoking," I reply in a slight panic.

"Hmmm, that's not good. What color was the smoke?"

"What do you mean 'what color was the smoke'? It was smoke. I didn't know car smoke came in Technicolor." "Yes, it does" he explained. "if its white smoke, ya got a blown head gasket, or maybe a manifold leak. If ya got blue smoke, you're burning oil in you're cylinders. Black smoke, ya got too much gas in the mix." Looking at the mechanic with a dropped jaw, tears in my eyes and a pit in my stomach I am now wishing I had more to eat today than just a cup of tea. "Let's take a look," he says as he pops the hood.

"Well, it appears you blew a head gasket," he says as he continues his examination of my poor, sad engine.

I blew a what? What's a gasket? If this is a head gasket, does this mean there are other gaskets in there as well, such as an arm gasket or a leg gasket? I quietly ask myself.

"How much is this going to cost?" I nervously inquire.

Coming out from under the hood he says, "Fixing a blown gasket can cost you anywhere between $1,100 and $1,700, but I'll have to take a closer look and let you know. Have a seat in the waiting room." I walk unsteadily toward the waiting room thinking of my finances or lack thereof. I wonder if hitchhiking is really as unsafe as people say.

The stark waiting room smells like grease and stale coffee and is filled with nothing but Sports Illustrated and MotorTrend magazines. The receptionist is filing her nails and snapping her gum. I wonder how much she is being paid to do nothing and if they would like a replacement; I have an extra copy of my resume in the car with the white smoke. I sit and silently say a small prayer that it's going to cost more toward the lower end of the quote and mentally tally how much or how little is in my checking account. A few minutes later the mechanic walks in shaking his head and confirms that it is the head gasket. He tells me the bad news is that it will cost me $1,350 including labor to fix. The good news is that he can have it done within the hour.

I suppose my prayer was answered. I suppose it could have been worse. And at least I didn't have to go through the expense of a rental car. Of course it could have been even better had this not happened at all.

I hand over my credit card which I carry just for emergencies and say another prayer that I have enough funds on there to get my car fixed.

Oh, why me? Why is this happening? And if it HAD to happen then why could it not have happened six months ago when I had a job and a steady income?

Again, I start to cry. Damn menopausal emotions.

OVER FIFTY? MENOPAUSAL? YOU'RE FIRED!!!

CHAPTER 12

The Long Wait

YEARS HAVE GONE BY AND I HAVEN'T HEARD ANYTHING FROM THE SWINDLE AND KONN CORPORATION SINCE MY INTERVIEW. Okay, so I exaggerated a little. It has been only two weeks but it feels like years.

I don't understand. Why does it take so long to make a decision? I know they have a lot of other people they are interviewing but the position isn't for a brain surgeon or for a spy with the CIA.

Waiting for the phone call or email stating that some human has actually read my resume and acknowledged my existence is unbearable. At this point, I feel like I'm a wallflower at the Annual Sock Hop waiting for someone to ask me to dance. I'm in my prettiest dress sitting up straight in a hard chair surrounded by other girls in their prettiest dresses who are also waiting. We're all looking at the boys wondering, 'will he be the one to ask me to dance or will it be that one or maybe that other one or maybe no one.' I just have to wait and see.

Didn't Tom Petty and the Heartbreakers write a song called *The Waiting is the Hardest Part?* Do you suppose he wrote that song because at one time he too was out of a job and had to wait for someone to determine his future? Probably not, but the waiting IS the hardest part. Every morning I wake up wondering if today I'll get the call that they want to hire me. Every morning I wake up wondering if today is the day I no longer have to apply to more job postings and I can finally get a good night's sleep.

Again, I search the internet for other opportunities.

Ah! Here's one! A law firm is looking for an Executive Assistant with 10+ years of experience, and has extensive knowledge using the Cook and Done 250 machine and the AJ 2100 Phone System. OMG, this is perfect for me. I see that it's located only 15 minutes from my house too. The name of the firm is called Alibye and Meanor LLC. Hmmm… I never heard of them but I don't care. They have a need for someone like me and I am the perfect person to fill it!

I fill out the online application, careful to follow the instructions perfectly. I finish, say a little prayer, cross every body part that can be crossed, and press the SUBMIT button.

And now I wait. …**AGAIN!**

Not more than an hour passes and the phone rings. It's the law firm of Alibye and Meanor LLC. They received my resume and they want me to come in this afternoon for an interview.

Excitedly, but not too excitedly, I accept and we agree to meet at 4 p.m. I thank them, hang up the phone and start to cry. Am I crying because I'm afraid? Am I crying because I'm happy? Or, am I crying because my hormones are all mixed up? I think it's a combination of all three.

I dress professionally and arrive as scheduled leaving a few minutes to go into the restroom to freshen up.

I see the beautiful glass double doors with the letter A etched on one door and M etched on the other, both in an elegant font.

Keeping my head up and shoulders back I greet the receptionist and tell her I'm here for a 4 p.m. interview.

She welcomes me and asks me if I would like any coffee, water or soda. I thank her but decline. My hands are shaking so much I would probably spill the drink before reaching my mouth. She leads me into a large, warm paneled conference room where two women are already seated. Both women stand and extend their hand.

"I am Anita Alibye and this is my law partner Misty Meanor. We are so glad you were able to meet with us on such short notice."

I inconspicuously wipe my moist palms on the back of my skirt, shake their hands and all three of us sit. "So, Penny. We are looking for someone who can handle a busy law office and manage both of our schedules. We are defense attorneys specializing in criminal law. We are very particular about our clientele and only represent those whom we feel were truly wronged by extenuating circumstances and just plain being in the wrong place at the wrong time. Our practice has been around for over 20 years and we've attained a very favorable and respected reputation among our clients and colleagues. This is an extremely fast-paced environment and it's imperative that all stated deadlines are met. Missing a deadline can mean that a case may be thrown out or some evidence may not be allowed to be presented."

"Does this sounds like the kind of position that may interest you?"

Hoping the sound of my heart pounding and the rush of adrenalin racing through my body doesn't scare them off I reply, "Yes, this describes my personality and work ethic to a tee. I am meticulous about deadlines and extremely organized. At my last job they called me 'Proactive Penny' because I always had everything in order, in its place and ready when needed."

Proactive Penny? Ugh. How lame. Now they are going to think I'm someone with an OCD disorder–who sweats a lot!

66

I continue. "In my last three jobs, I was solely responsible for the busy and ever-changing schedules of the CEO, CFO and CIO. They constantly ran from place to place and meeting to meeting. They relied on me to tell them where they needed to go, who would be there and to have everything they needed to do whatever it was they were doing. It was fast-paced but I really enjoyed the challenge and they were happy to have me in their corner."

Way to blow your own horn, Penny. You go, girl!

"How do you feel about working for a firm who defends clients who may have already been accused of a crime?" Anita Alibye asks.

Funny she asked that question. I was just thinking that this firm will be great at defending me because there are several people at the Weadont Care Company I'd like to knock off. "I have no problem working with defendants. I believe everyone deserves a fair trial."

"Well, this sounds great, Penny. Of course, we have a few other candidates we need to interview as well. Thank you for coming in to speak to us," Misty Meanor states as she and Anita Alibye stand and once again extended their hand. "We will make our decision and get back with you soon." Like clockwork, the receptionist who showed me in appears to now show me out.

I think I did okay. Should I have said more about my knowledge of organization or maybe I should have said less about my passion for thoroughness? Did I come across as confident or did I sound desperate? Did I appear professional or did I seem too rigid?

Sighhh.

As soon as I am home I take off my heels, panty hose, suit and unpretentious jewelry and wrap myself into my well-worn but comfy jammies.

I grab a big bowl of cookie-dough ice cream, accent it with sprinkles and a little whipped topping, turn on one of my favorite shows and settle myself into my always-welcoming easy chair. I deserve this. I'm mentally exhausted.

I must have fallen asleep, because when I awake the next morning, the TV is still on but now showing some infomercial about how to improve your sex life. *Sex life? I would kill for just a date!* I promptly turn it off and drag myself into the shower.

Feeling refreshed, I whip out my laptop and start checking my emails. Surely I should hear by now the decision regarding the Swindle and Konn Corporation position. Maybe the law firm of Alibye and Meanor LLC made their decision. But no, there are no emails from either company.

The waiting is excruciating. I'm on pins and needles every day. I jump every time the phone rings and I pounce on my laptop every time I get a notification that I received new email.

I make myself a healthy breakfast. It's important to keep your health in tip-top shape just in case you get that coveted acceptance call. I get dressed and go about my day running meaningless errands, networking with people just like me and searching the job boards.

OVER FIFTY? MENOPAUSAL? YOU'RE FIRED!!!

CHAPTER 13
The Offer

I'M IN MY CAR ON MY WAY HOME FROM ONE OF MY DAILY ERRANDS WHEN SUDDENLY MY CELL PHONE RINGS. IT'S A NUMBER I DON'T RECOGNIZE.

"Hello?" I answer with a question in my voice.

"Hello Penny, this is Anita Alibye. Misty and I were very impressed with you at our last meeting. We would like to offer you a position with our firm."

At this point I almost drive off the road. I am so excited I can't contain myself. I pull over to a nearby parking lot and throw the gear shift to Park. I simultaneously direct the A/C vents toward my face as another hot flash begins to roast me from inside out.

Anita continues, "We can offer you the salary that we discussed as well as two weeks paid vacation after six months and full medical/dental/vision benefits beginning after 30 days. Our only criteria is that you start next Monday. How does that work for you?" I cannot believe what I'm hearing. I try not to panic. I try to sound calm and collected as if this is one of many offers I've received today. "Yes, that will work for me and yes, I am able to start next Monday." I would have blown through every red light between here and their office if they wanted me right now!!

"I'm excited about joining your firm. Thank you."

"Well, thank you Penny. We'll do all the paperwork once you're here. We look forward to seeing you at 8:30 a.m. sharp next Monday. Bye." And there it is. The moment that all unemployed people strive for:

THE OFFER!!!

It's the Olympic gold medal, the Super Bowl ring, the Blue Ribbon for best apple pie, the Academy Award, the Miss America sash, the Triple Crown, the World Series championship, the Pulitzer Prize for the unemployed. It represents that you have been accepted, that you are wanted, that you are needed and that someone is willing to pay you for your skills and talents. This is your Hall of Fame moment.

Somehow, I manage to drive home safely. I have to tell someone, anyone, everyone. I want to shout it from the rooftops. The first person I call is my BFF Wanda Working. She is so happy for me and we're both laughing and crying at the same time. We make a plan to get together this weekend to celebrate.

But wait! I'm sweating; my heart is racing; I'm in panic mode. What if they change their mind between now and Monday? What if a more qualified candidate comes into their office? What if they take these few days and come to the realization that maybe I'm NOT the best fit?

On the other hand, what if the Swindle and Konn Corporation calls and gives me an offer as well? What do I do? Do I go with the Swindle and Konn Corporation or do I go with Alibye and Meanor, LLC? Do I go with the company who is paying me the most with the best benefits or the company that I feel more comfortable?

What if, what if, what if…? What do I do, what do I do, what do I do…?

Monday couldn't come fast enough. I was ready for the first day of my new job the same afternoon as when I received the offer. I dress in the appropriate attire and bring all of my important documents required when starting a new job. The receptionist at Alibye and Meanor LLC greets me warmly and shows me to my desk. She asks me to take a few minutes to settle in and she'll return to introduce me to the other staff members and show me around the office. I couldn't be more excited if I had won the lottery. Landing this job is just like winning the lottery except I was specifically and personally chosen and not selected by chance.

Later that morning, Anita Alibye and Misty Meanor come by my desk to say hello and to brief me on what's to be expected. They couldn't be more gracious and kind.

This is going to be a wonderful and joyous employment. I can't wait to see what my future holds at Alibye and Meanor LLC.

OVER FIFTY? MENOPAUSAL? YOU'RE FIRED!!!

CHAPTER 14

The Circle of (Unemployment) Life

IT'S BEEN ABOUT NINE MONTHS NOW AND I FEEL SO HAPPY AND COMFORTABLE. I've worked hard to learn Anita and Misty's hectic schedules and ensure they are on time at all times. I've constructed a method of keeping up with all court deadlines and I've reorganized the office so that current cases are easier to find. I'm on cloud nine and I feel at home.

Since my employment, I've made many friends and have enjoyed several after-work outings with them. I've participated in a few company holiday events and I even got a chance to bake one of my famous pumpkin pies that everyone seemed to love.

Three months into my employment, I finally receive a rejection letter from Swindle and Konn Corporation. Getting a rejection of any kind is heart wrenching but this one made me laugh. Another funny thing happened after about five months of my new employment. The Weadont Care Company called, wanting me to come back. It seems they had a reorganization of the reorganization; they now have a place for me

and they need me to return to my previously held position. *Thanks but no thanks, too little too late,* I think to myself with a smile. I respectfully decline the offer. I'm in a much better place but it sure was nice having them pursue me. As I hang up the phone I think to myself, *Sweet Karma, what goes around comes around, and this time it's in my favor.*

One evening while I'm home after a long day, my cell phone rings. It is my BFF Wanda Working. Her voice is frantic.

"I was just laid off! I am over fifty. Who will want me? What should I do?"

"Come right over," I tell her.

While waiting for Wanda, I run to my home-office and open the huge paper box filled with unemployment information; contact names, important phone numbers, business websites… Everything we need. Except one thing.

Pushing all the paperwork aside, I keep digging.

Found it! The one item that helped me the most; a self–help book titled, *Over Fifty? Menopausal? You're Fired!!!*

Wanda arrives at my house in record time. I give her a big hug and a crucial glass of wine. "Everything will be fine," I tell her.

I crank down the A/C to deter the inevitable hot flashes, and we head off to the kitchen to talk.

I hand Wanda the prized book. She flips through a few pages. Her eyes widen. "This is GREAT! Where did you get this?" We continue to read and read and read some more.

"This is exactly what I need." A smile spreads across Wanda's face as she gives me another hug.

She now has two rocks to lean on; me and this book.

Once again, another victim of unemployment has new hopes and dreams.

The circle of unemployment life continues.

Tomorrow is a new beginning.

OVER FIFTY? MENOPAUSAL? YOU'RE FIRED!!!

Notes:

_____

_____

_____

_____

_____

_____

_____

_____

_____

_____

CPSIA information can be obtained
at www.ICGtesting.com
Printed in the USA
LVOW05s0929231217
560536LV00010BA/652/P

9 781944 952129